Diamond Elite Magazine

1st Quarter 2018

"A different type of magazine"

Content:

- Pg. 3 QueenLifee-Hair Tips 101
- Pg. 4 Team Glam Paparazzi
- Pg. 5 Shawn Starling Collection
- Pg. 6 Featured 1st QTR Books
- Pg. 7 Morning Coffee
- Pg. 8 DDT It!
- Pg. 9 K&K Publishing
- Pg. 10 New Year New Goals
- Pg. 11 Elissa Mitchell
- Pg. 12 You MVP
- Pg.13-14 Vision Board
- Pg. 16 Stream with Shakala
- Pg. 17 Rejected & Rich
- Pg. 19 Writing Submissions
- Pg. 20 Infinite Solutions Cleaning
- Pg. 21-22 When Out and About
- Pg. 23 Reality Speaks

Mission Statement:

Diamond Elite Magazine's goal is to boost the exposure and sales of entrepreneurs. We believe networking word of mouth are the biggest essentials when it comes to small business. As the years continue, we plan to thrive in success and help expand the small businesses who have contributed along the way.

Diamond Elite — The Magazine for Small Business

CHEERS TO 2018!

It is a new year, which means new starts, new goals, new journeys, new trends. New-New-New.

Each day this year, stop and think if you are doing the best you can in that very moment at least once each day. Become a better you!

-Founder
Kandice Iglehart-Jarrett

Are you living the QueenLifee or Are You Just Another Pretty Face?

Top Quality Bundles at an Affordable Price

Brazilian Bundles starting at $50 | Mink Brazilian Bundles starting at $65

@QueenLifeeHair www.queenlifeehair.com @QueenLifeeHair_

- It is best to use satin or silk pillowcases. Cotton pillows cause breakage.
- Shampoo your scalp-Condition your hair!
- Choose whether you are going to flat iron or blow-dry your hair. Avoid doing both!
- After washing your hair, avoid combing or brushing until dry. Hair is weaker and brittle while wet.

Team Glam Paparazzi

Do you love to accessorize and glamorize in addition to sticking to your budget? Team Glam Paparazzi $5 Accessories are always fabulous, always fashionable, always fun and always $5! New inventory is added daily and our variety insures that there is something for every taste. Shop online at

www.teamglampaparazzi.com

Check out our opportunity to earn extra income by becoming a consultant, too!

For more information, contact us at teamglampaparazzi@yahoo.com

Shawn Starling Collection

  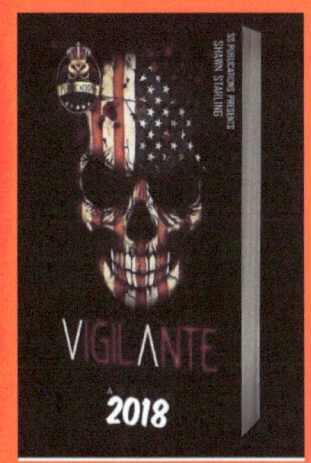 

Pen in the Pen
PUBLISHING

A publishing company based out of New Jersey devoted to publishing various genres of books & poetry for the incarcerated.

If you would like us to send brochures to your loved one, please contact us via email with their Name, ID Number, Facility Name, and Address.

peninthepenpublishing@gmail.com

USE CODE "FREEDOM" for 10% OFF a Basic Publishing Package.

pen in the pen
PUBLISHING
PO BOX 4092
LONG BRANCH, NJ
PENINTHEPEN.COM

Featured 1st Quarter Books

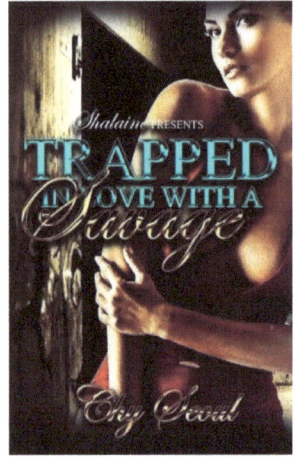

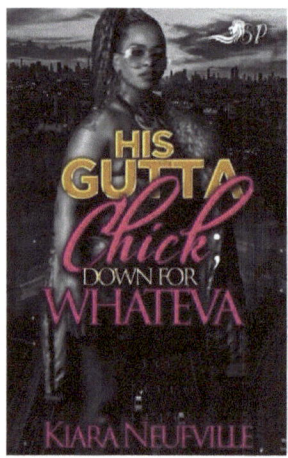

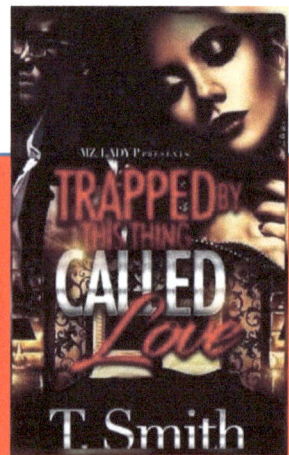
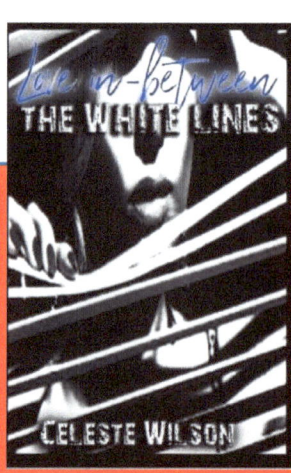

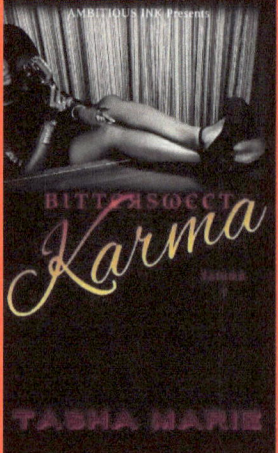
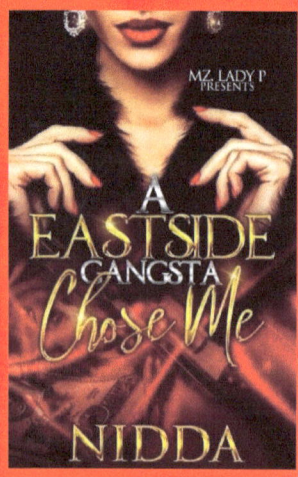

AVAILABLE NOW!

Morning Coffee
...the book that's filled with romance, love, and sensuality…& MORE!

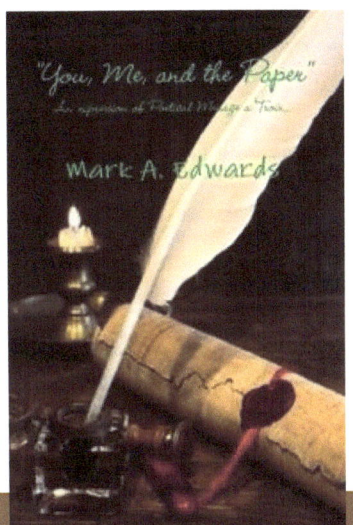

Available at
lulu.com/spotlight/MEdwards

Coffee Facts

-Espresso is regulated by the Italian government because it is considered to be an essential part of their daily life.

-Coffee beans are actually the pit of a berry, which makes them a fruit.

Buy Morning Coffee
By Mark Edwards
to Fulfill Your Morning.

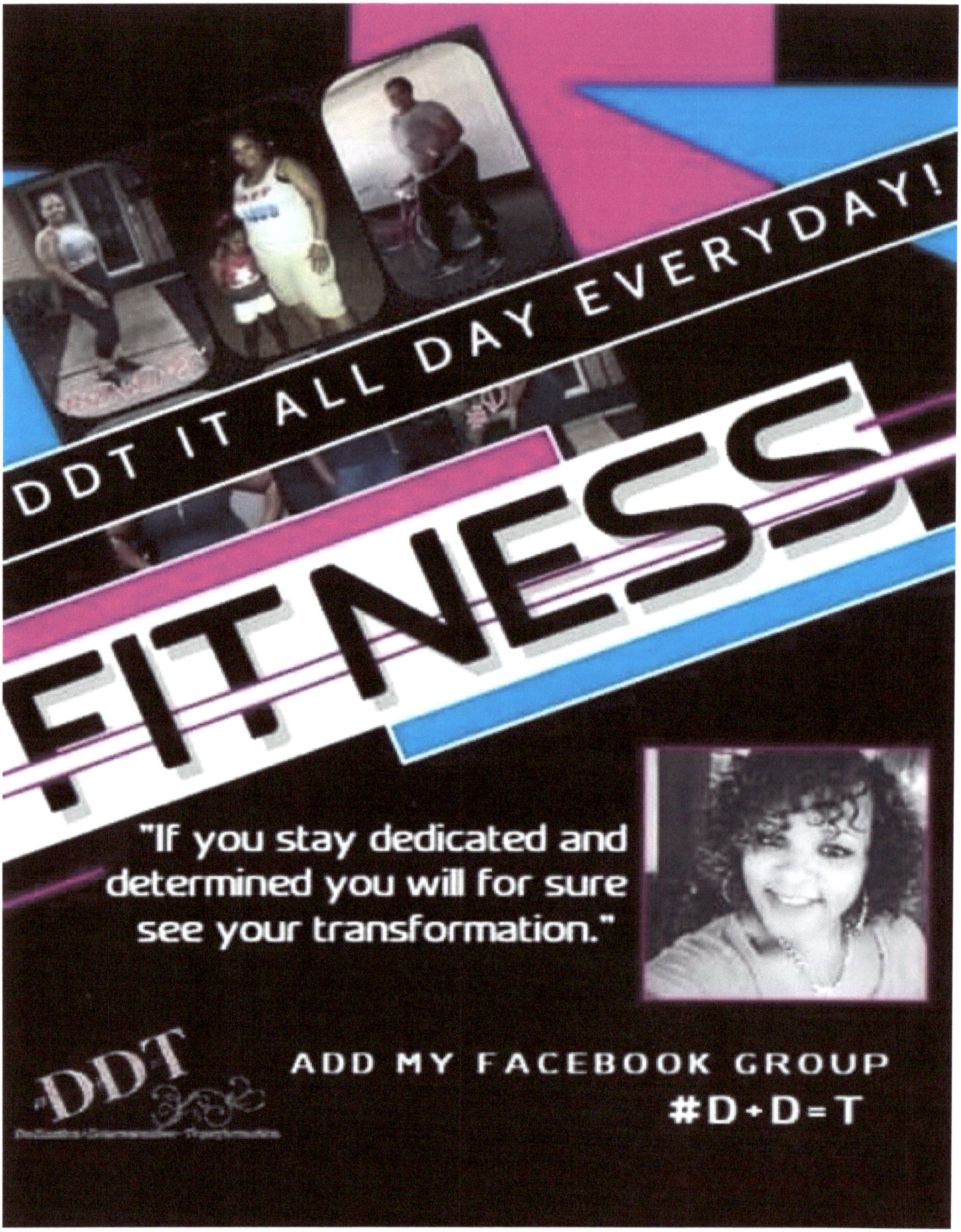
DDT IT ALL DAY EVERYDAY!
FITNESS
"If you stay dedicated and determined you will for sure see your transformation."
DDT
ADD MY FACEBOOK GROUP
#D+D=T

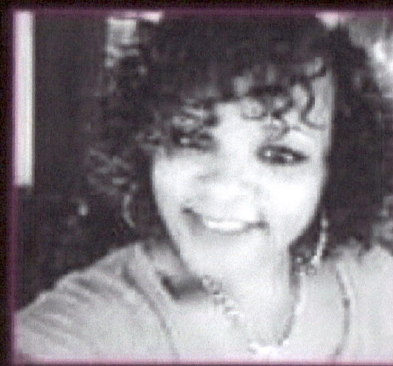

...Join K&K Publishing

One-Time Fee Upfront
We do: Editing, Formatting, Copyrights, Illustrations (ALL for You!)
60/40 Royalties
Your Book will be in Select Independent Bookstores
Online Retailers: Barnes & Noble, Amazon, BAM! etc.
Contact us Today! Email k_kpublishing@yahoo.com

"Like" on Facebook! *A Select Variety of Styles*

NEW YEAR

During the new year there is a certain tactic most of us do, and that is to have new goals for the new year. We may come to the conclusion that what we did the previous year needs to be switched up in some form or fashion...because obviously certain goals weren't reached.

Furthermore, we begin to look at the individuals around us. This may include our spouses, siblings, kids, or even friends and wonder if they were the cause. Then we tend to look at our occupation and believe maybe that is the issue.

Rarely do we take the time out just to look in the mirror to analyze ourselves and what we can do differently to avoid the same approach next year.

New Year. New Goals. New You.

NEW GOALS

Meet Elissa Mitchell

Elissa Mitchell always had a passion to write since being a young girl in the 4th grade. She would write many short stories and works of non-fiction. Later in her 20's she began writing poetry, which was a way for her to relax and escape her environment. When asked her favorite author, she answered with Bishop T.D. Jakes. She stated she relates to his writings on a spiritual realm. She is a true follower of his teachings, and enjoys that most of his books are good for entrepreneurs as well as a quick read.

Mitchell became interested in the literary industry when she was exploring network marketing, one of the best things for her to do was to stand out, and what better way than becoming a part of a book? Her debut novel, "You Have No Idea the Hell I've Been Through" is a collaboration book with other women. Their mission of this book is to bring hope to millions of men and women out there in the world by giving the notion of hope. The concept behind the book is from Taurea Avant, she is a Business Educator with an online university to teach small business owners how to write a book in 30 days and leverage the book into your business to create multiple stream of income. "You Have No Idea the Hell I've Been Through" shares stories of childhood, life challenges, battles, disappointments, and abuse. The women then share what they are doing now in life to help others in similar circumstances.

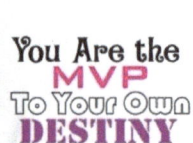

https://elitegemsinc.wixsite.com/youmvp

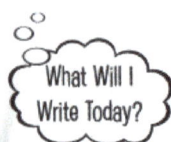

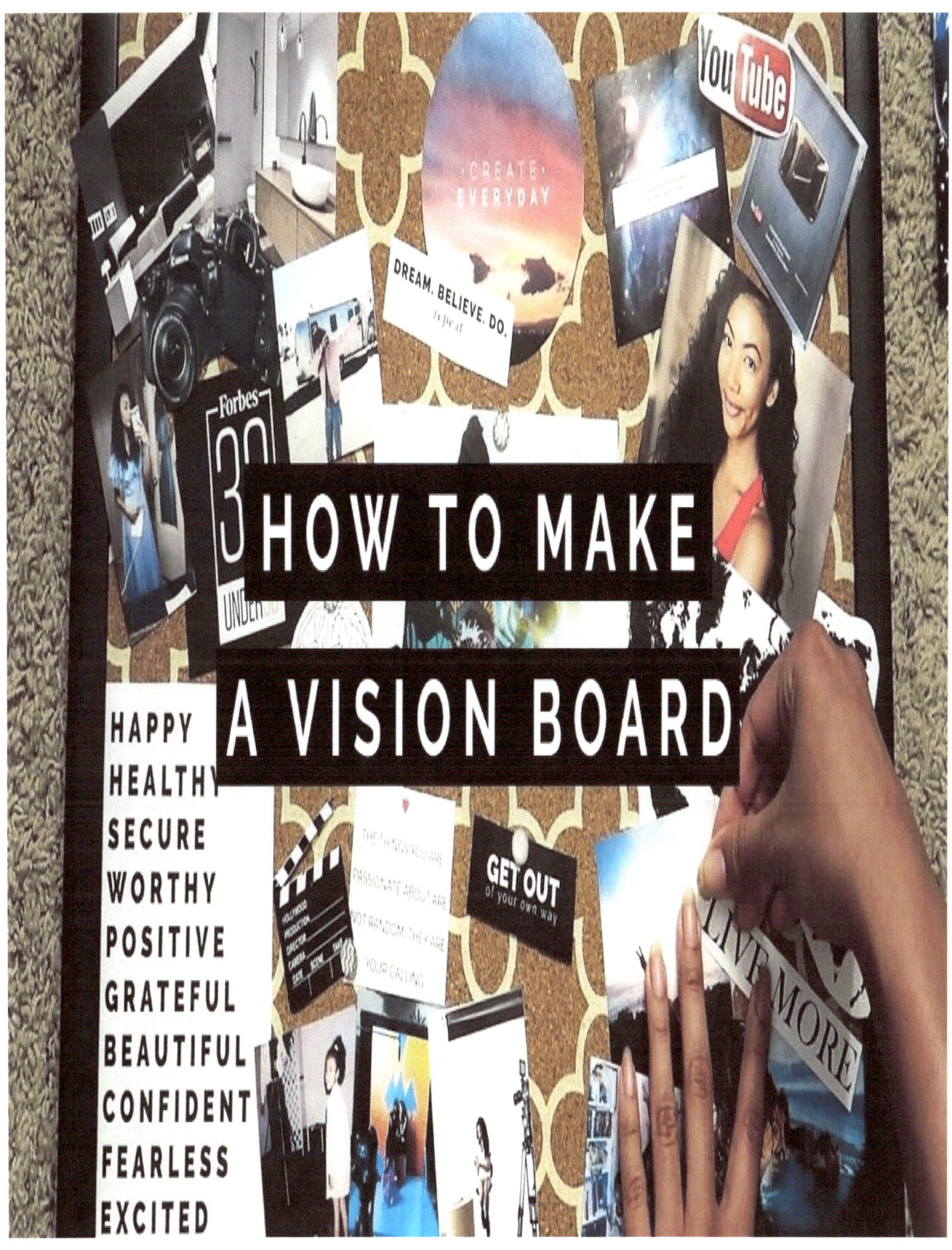

VISION BOARD BLUES

- **Gather Magazines**
- **Gather Supplies**
- **Brainstorm**
  - **Goals**
  - **Traveling**
  - **Finances**
- **Ready, Set, CUT!**
- **Paste or Pin to a Board!**

The GOAL is to make the DREAM a REALITY!

Services Include:

Mobile Services
Protective Services
Home Services
Electric Service

Contact Me Today!
254-229-1301
shakalajefferson@gmail.com
www.shakalaj.mystream.com

The **Infamous** Stories Of the Rejected & RICH!

J.K. Rowling

The great literary success story, failed to sell *Harry Potter and the Philosopher's Stone* to 12 different publishers until the daughter of an editor at Bloomsbury Publishing took an interest in it. Harry Potter is now worth at least $15 billion.

Dr. Seuss

suffered through 27 rejections when trying to sell his first story. He gave the credit for finally selling *And To Think That I Saw It On Mulberry Street* to the sheer dumb luck of running into a friend who worked in publishing on the street.

Judy Blume

got nothing but rejections for the first two years of her writing career. She says the rejections from *Highlights for Children* were so embarrassing that the sight of a copy of *Highlights* still makes her wince.

Kathryn Stockett

was turned down by 60 literary agents before she found someone willing to represent *The Help*. "Three weeks later," she says, "we sold the book." *The Help* later spent 100 weeks on the *New York Times* bestseller list.

Never give up. Today is hard, tomorrow will be worse, but the day after tomorrow will be sunshine.

—Jack Ma

2018 Writing Submissions

Please be advised this is not a Paid Opportunity

Would You Like to Write for Diamond Elite Magazine?

Information:

Word Count: 500-1000 Words

Topics: Leadership, Entrepreneurship, Inspiration

Please Include: Picture, Website/Blog, Social Media Account Names

Please email submission to **diamondelitemagazine@yahoo.com**

Please be aware that your article will may be edited and formatted to our discretion. It is not automatically subject to be included in our magazine. You will receive an email if approved or declined.

Infinite Solutions Cleaning Services

Insured and Bonded

"The cleaning service where quality service never ends!"

CALL US TO BOOK AN APPOINTMENT

469-996-4296

Infinite Solutions Cleaning Services

Follow Us on Facebook!

When Out & About

Something Special Styling Salon

3317 Finley Rd. Suite #230

Irving, TX 75062

The Barber Lounge for Men

11850 Park Waldorf Ln. Ste 107

Waldorf, MD 20601

A Touch of Class Beauty Salon
1300 W Waco Dr
Waco, Tx 76701

Do you have an establishment that wouldn't mind carrying Diamond Elite Magazine copies for your patrons? Please reach out and let us know by visiting **www.diamondelitemagazine.com**

GOT ADVERTISEMENT?

IF YOU WOULD LIKE TO BE APART OF THE DIAMOND ELITE FAMILY PLEASE VISIT OUR WEBSITE.

WWW.DIAMONDELITEMAGAZINE.COM

www.ingramcontent.com/pod-product-compliance
Lightning Source LLC
Chambersburg PA
CBHW051836210526
45473CB00005B/1895